LOVE or LONELINESS
you decide...

Dr. Robert H. Schuller

LOVE or LONELINESS you decide...

Hour of Power Publishers
Garden Grove, California 92642

This book is dedicated to the loyal staff and faithful volunteers who help me in my ministry. They are truly instruments of Christ's love, healing the loneliness in the hearts of people.

FOREWORD

Recently, one of our Hour of Power listeners, Abigail Van Buren, known to many of you as "Dear Abby," was talking to me. We agreed that the bulk of our mail indicates that there are multiplied tens of millions of Americans who are desperate for acceptance, understanding, and love.

People who are hungry for self-worth, and for acceptance by others, need an experience of authentic love.

This powerful, helpful love is defined in the Bible in I Corinthians, Chapter 13.

I know of no other chapter in the Bible — unless it would be the 23rd Psalm — that has been so meaningful in revolutionizing human lives as this great chapter on love in the Holy Bible.

For several months I delivered messages on this chapter to my national television audience. The response was overwhelming. We have, accordingly, selected those messages that were in greatest demand and herewith offer them as a unity of HOPE — for you.

Here's a tremendous suggestion. Read this "greatest chapter in the Bible" once a day for a month. And see what a miracle you'll experience!

Yours in Christ's happy service!

Robert Schuller

CONTENTS

Foreword   11

Chapter One: 20
LOVE IS THE GREATEST
"... but the greatest of these is love."
(I Cor. 13:13)

Chapter Two: 34
LOVE — THE FORCE THAT PUTS POWER IN FAITH
"Love believes all things."
(I Cor. 13:7)

Chapter Three: 44
COMPROMISE CAN BE KINGLY
"Love seeketh not her own."
(I Cor. 13:5)

Chapter Four: 54
LIVING BEYOND THE POSSIBILITY OF PERSONAL FAILURE
"Love never fails."
(I Cor. 13:8)

Chapter Five: 64
HERE'S A LOVE TO END YOUR LONELINESS
"So faith, hope, love abide, these three; but the greatest of these is love."
(I Cor. 13:13)

Chapter Six: 76
"I FORGIVE YOU": THE LANGUAGE OF LOVE
"Love is not resentful."
(I Cor. 13:5)

Chapter Seven: 86
HOW YOU CAN HAVE THE POWER TO COPE
"Love endures all things."
(I Cor. 13:7)

Chapter Eight: 98
LOVE CONOUERS FEAR
"There is no fear in love."
(I John 4:18)

13

*Here is
real love . . .*

THOUGH I speak with the tongues of men and of angels, and have not charity, I am become as sounding brass, or a tinkling cymbal.

2 And though I have the gift of prophecy, and understand all mysteries, and all knowledge; and though I have all faith, so that I could remove mountains, and have not charity, I am nothing.

3 And though I bestow all my goods to feed the poor, and though I give my body to be burned, and have not charity, it profiteth me nothing.

4 Charity suffereth long, and is kind; charity envieth not; charity vaunteth not itself, is not puffed up,

5 Doth not behave itself unseemly, seeketh not her own, is not easily provoked, thinketh no evil;

6 Rejoiceth not in iniquity, but rejoiceth in the truth;

7 Beareth all things, believeth all things, hopeth all things, endureth all things.

8 Charity never faileth: but whether there be prophecies, they shall fail; whether there be tongues, they shall cease; whether there be knowledge, it shall vanish away.

9 For we know in part, and we prophesy in part.

10 But when that which is perfect is come, then that which is in part shall be done away.

11 When I was a child, I spake as a child, I understood as a child, I thought as a child: but when I became a man, I put away childish things.

12 For now we see through a glass, darkly; but then face to face: now I know in part; but then shall I know even as also I am known.

13 And now abideth faith, hope, charity, these three; but the greatest of these is charity.

I Corinthians, Chapter 13
(*King James Translation*)

IF I SPEAK in the tongues of men and of angels, but have not love, I am a noisy gong or a clanging cymbal. 2 And if I have prophetic powers, and understand all mysteries and all knowledge, and if I have all faith, so as to remove mountains, but have not love, I am nothing. 3 If I give away all I have, and if I deliver my body to be burned, but have not love, I gain nothing. 4 Love is patient and kind; love is not jealous or boastful; 5 it is not arrogant or rude. Love does not insist on its own way; it is not irritable or resentful; 6 it does not rejoice at wrong, but rejoices in the right. 7 Love bears all things, believes all things, hopes all things, endures all things. 8 Love never ends; as for prophecies, they will pass away; as for tongues, they will cease; as for knowledge, it will pass away. 9 For our knowledge is imperfect and our prophecy is imperfect; 10 but when the perfect comes, the imperfect will pass away. 11 When I was a child, I spoke like a child, I thought like a child, I reasoned like a child; when I became a man, I gave up childish ways. 12 For now we see in a mirror dimly, but then face to face. Now I know in part; then I shall understand fully, even as I have been fully understood. 13 So faith, hope, love abide, these three; but the greatest of these is love.

I Corinthians, Chapter 13
(*Revised Standard Translation*)

IF I SPEAK with the eloquence of men and of angels, but have no love, I become no more than blaring brass or crashing cymbal. If I have the gift of foretelling the future and hold in my mind not only all human knowledge but the very secrets of God, and if I have that absolute faith which can move mountains, but have no love, I amount to nothing at all. If I dispose of all that I possess, yes, even if I give my own body to be burned, but have no love, I achieve precisely nothing.

This love of which I speak is slow to lose patience — it looks for a way of being constructive. It is not possessive: it is neither anxious to impress nor does it cherish inflated ideas of its own importance.

Love has good manners and does not pursue selfish advantage. It is not touchy. It does not keep account of evil or gloat over the wickedness of other people. On the contrary, it is glad with all good men when truth prevails.

Love knows no limit to its endurance, no end to its trust, no fading of its hope; it can outlast anything. It is, in fact, the one thing that still stands when all else has fallen.

For if there are prophecies they will be fulfilled and done with, if there are "tongues" the need for them will disappear, if there is knowledge it will be swallowed up in truth. For our knowledge is always incomplete and our prophecy is always incomplete, and when the complete comes, that is the end of the incomplete.

When I was a little child I talked and felt and thought like a little child. Now that I am a man my childish speech and feeling and thought have no further significance for me.

At present we are men looking at puzzling reflections in a mirror. The time will come when we shall see reality whole and face to face! At present all I know is a little fraction of the truth, but the time will come when I shall know it as fully as God now knows me!

In this life we have three great lasting qualities — faith, hope and love. But the greatest of them is love.

I Corinthians, Chapter 13
(Phillips Translation)

If I had the gift of being able to speak in other languages without learning them, and could speak in every language there is in all of heaven and earth, but didn't love others, I would only be making noise.

2 If I had the gift of prophecy and knew all about what is going to happen in the future, knew everything about everything, but didn't love others, what good would it do? Even if I had the gift of faith so that I could speak to a mountain and make it move, I would still be worth nothing at all without love.

3 If I gave everything I have to poor people, and if I were burned alive for preaching the Gospel but didn't love others, it would be of no value whatever.

4 Love is very patient and kind, never jealous or envious, never boastful or proud.

5 Never haughty or selfish or rude. Love does not demand its own way. It is not irritable or touchy. It does not hold grudges and will hardly even notice when others do it wrong.

6 It is never glad about injustice, but rejoices whenever truth wins out.

7 If you love someone you will be loyal to him no matter what the cost. You will always believe in him, always expect the best of him, and always stand your ground in defending him.

8 All the special gifts and powers from God will someday come to an end, but love goes on forever. Someday prophecy, and speaking unknown languages, and special knowledge — these gifts will disappear.

9 Now we know so little, even with our special gifts, and the preaching of those most gifted is still so poor.

10 But when we have been made perfect and complete, then the need for these inadequate special gifts will come to an end, and they will disappear.

11 It's like this: when I was a child I spoke and thought and reasoned as a child does. But when I became a man my thoughts grew far beyond those of my childhood, and now I have put away the childish things.

12 In the same way, we can see and understand only a little about God now, as if we were peering at His reflection in a poor mirror; but someday we are going to see Him in His completeness, face to face. Now all that I know is hazy and blurred, but then I will see everything clearly, just as clearly as God sees into my heart right now.

13 There are three things that remain — faith, hope, and love — and the greatest of these is love.

I Corinthians, Chapter 13
(Living Translation)

CHAPTER ONE

No Problem
is too big for
God's Power;
No Person
is too small for
God's Love.

" . . . but the greatest of these is love."
(I Cor. 13:13)

I

Love Is The Greatest

" . . . but the greatest of these is love."

"If there is one thing that is sure and certain, it is that nothing is sure and certain." That, at least, is what the cynic would say. The cynic would tell us that change and decay are all around us and that this is the one and only certainty. And, of course, that is the great paradox. If the only thing that is certain is change, then nothing is certain.

Well, the good news I have for you is this: *There is something that does not change!* And that something is man — you and me and every man. Everybody who is born, everybody who lives and everybody who dies, every human being all around the world is the same, and he doesn't change. His basic needs do not change. Every human being who is born needs to eat, breathe and drink water, or he will die. The body does not change in its demands. And the heart of man does not change. Every heart needs the food of human love.

What is that deep yearning in your heart? Are there times when your heart almost seems moist in its crying out for nourishment? What is it that you need deep down in your soul?

Have you felt a restlessness within your heart? You know what it's like to feel hungry. The stomach seems empty and it craves and calls for food. Have you had something like that as far as your heart is concerned? Psychologists call it, of course, being emotionally deprived. We use the words *heart hunger.* The heart has a constant hunger for love. Nothing else satisfies. It's like going to a refrigerator and opening it and wondering what you're hungry for. You see this and you see that, and you finally take a nibble and go to bed still unsatisfied, not knowing what you really wanted. That hungry, craving restlessness — your heart has it. It's really a mark of health. A body that doesn't have a physical appetite is sick. And if you don't have that constant recurring restlessness of a hunger in your heart, then you're not healthy. That recurring restlessness of the heart's hunger is a heart's call for the food of love.

Long before this youthful science called Psychiatry (and it is only a half century old), there was a book, a book called the Bible. And it said, man's body needs food and drink, and man's heart needs love. And if it does not have love, that heart will be undernourished. It will cry out for nutrition. How it cries out — you know. Look around you at the world!

The good news I have for you is that you do not change, I do not change, the Bible does not change and God does not change. Your heart needs love and God is able to give it to you. And God has set things up in such a way that you can get it.

Recently Mrs. Schuller and I and my two little girls spent a few days at a mountain cabin we have high up in the California mountains, a place we built many, many years ago when things were still cheap! My littlest girl came to me one morning and said, "Daddy, in our Daily Vacation Bible School we were taught that if you take a pine cone and put peanut butter on it and you sprinkle bird seed on it, the bird seed will stick to the peanut butter, and you can put the pine cone out and little birds will eat the seed from the pine cone." I said to her, "You don't have to go through all that rigmarole. We've got some bird seed up in the cabin. Just put it right on the deck, and the birds will come up and eat it. You don't need to put it on peanut butter and on a pine cone and all of that." I gave her some bird seed, she put it on the railing of our deck, and sure enough, the bluejays came and gobbled it down, and the squirrels came and they gobbled it down. The jays fought with the squirrels and they all fought with each other, but they all got a stomach full. "I still think it would be nice to put it on a pine cone," my daughter persisted. It sounded like a nice project, so I finally gave in.

We went for a walk in the woods, and under one of the great old trees in the forest we found some pine cones and took them home. I tied a rope on the very top little prong of the cone so that I could tie it on the branch of a tree. Then we got out the peanut butter. What a mess trying to get peanut butter on and inside all of these little prongs! Then she sprinkled the bird seed on it, and sure enough, all the bird seed that hit the peanut butter stuck. But what didn't hit the peanut butter didn't stick, and it rolled like miniature marbles all over the decking where it crunched under our shoes for days later.

Finally she got it all speckled with bird seed. We took it outdoors and she tied it on a branch, right on the tip, so it hung down draping the branch, like a too-heavy ornament on the tender tip of a Christmas tree. "Gretchen," I said, "you should tie it in the solid middle." "No," she said, "I'll tie it here at the end." So she left it hanging at the end. Pretty soon the bluejays came, but they just flew around and didn't dare to land on the pine cone, because it was weaving back and forth and looked too unsteady for them; they didn't dare to sit on it. They stood on the branch, but they couldn't begin to get at it. They flew away in disgust. Pretty soon the squirrels came. They had smelled the peanut butter. Up the tree they went and onto the branch. I can still see that squirrel running down that branch, and as he's getting closer to the end, the branch starts to bend. He's just about to the spot where the rope is tied when the branch bends way down, and he backs off fearfully down the tree. What a lesson in frustration! He went up another branch, trying to approach it from the other way, but he was two feet away from it there. He ran down the railing and stuck his nose at it from there, but he was four feet away from it. Finally, in frustration, he ran off.

"Gretchen," I said, "it is a sublime failure. They can't eat it." And then it happened. All the *little birds* started coming. They came and literally walked down the rope and nibbled the food from the top so they wouldn't get their feet dirty with peanut butter. An amazing sight! Then more little birds came. One very resourceful possibility thinking winged creature grabbed the bottom of the pine cone where there was no peanut butter and he nibbled from the bottom. So the *little birds* had their feast, and the big bully bluejay and the big bully grey squirrel were left unfed. (But they didn't need it!)

Now what's the good news? Some of you people are poor. And you look at the very, very wealthy and you say, "God is unfair. They get it all, and I'm left with empty hands." The good news I have for you is this: As far as the food for your heart is concerned, God has set things up in such a way that the little people can always get what they need. The pine cone is set up so that the little birds are sure that they get what they need. And God has set this world in such a way that the little people can always get the love their hearts hunger for. We used this saying on our Hour of Power Calendar one year:

NO PROBLEM IS TOO BIG
FOR GOD'S POWER;
NO PERSON IS TOO SMALL
FOR GOD'S LOVE.

God loves you. And God is willing to fill your heart with that deep love. Love, the deepest need, is all over the world.

Awhile back a member of my staff calculated that I am a million miler. "What does that mean?" I asked. And he said, "You have flown over a million miles in your life." It sounded like an awful lot. "I think you're exaggerating," I told him. But he proved that it was not incorrect. I began thinking about it as I studied this chapter on Love. I really have travelled a lot. I have touched the pig - greased - covered naked bodies of what some people would call savages in the highlands of New Guinea, and deep in their expressive eyes I saw the same thing I see when I look into your eyes — love. And then I remember the bronzed, tan skin of the beautiful people who live in Shinaigar in the cool shadows of the Himalayas, not far from Nepal. There, living in their houseboats in the cool, high mountain lake are some of the most beautiful people in the world. Again, by our standards, poor and illiterate, uncultured, but what is culture without love?

St. Paul says in I Corinthians 13, if I'm eloquent and have the gift of tongues and do not have love, what good is eloquence? If I have oratorical ability, and do not have authentic love, it's nothing but a big show. If I have faith so that I can move mountains, but if I do not have love, then you'd better watch out, for faith without love is the most dangerous thing in the world.

This summer I was with a tour of eighty Hour of Power people. I want to say that it was one of the most enjoyable experiences of my life *for this reason,* (and this is a testimony): I've never been more excited than I am today, but I do not love my work more than I did the first three years that I was the pastor of my church, and I'll tell you why. I love people. I thrive on people. During the first three years after Mrs. Schuller and I started this church, I knew all the members by name, and I didn't have to think when I saw them coming. I didn't have to get tense inside and say, "Oh, what's their name, I can't remember it!" (Now I sometimes suffer from guilt and tension and miserable feelings because I can't remember everyone's name.)

I love people. This church is big. God has called me to a larger ministry and I can't know everybody's name, and I miss that more than you will ever know. So this summer we planned an Hour of Power tour, and we said we were going to limit it to eighty people. I had a reason for that. I was going to be on that tour, and I wanted to have only my tiny, little group so that I would know everybody's name. I was thrilled, because in twenty-four hours I knew everybody's name. So I was able to love every person personally!

Some years ago there was a musical on Broadway about a little girl who came down from the hills of Italy to join the circus. She said goodbye to her tiny little hometown called Mira. Lonesome, homesick, wandering through the quiet carnival tents, she started to sing this song: "What I like of Mira, is everybody knows my name. Yes, everybody knows my name. Now what do you think of that? Now what do you think of that? Yes, everybody knows my name."

I know that feeling. I was born in a town called Alton, Iowa. It was huge, I thought; it had 400 people. And I went to high school in Newkirk, Iowa. The total population of the high school was 73 when I was there. Our senior class had 14, which broke a record, the largest class in the history of Newkirk High School. They graduated me, and now they're out of business! They no longer exist!

Well, this summer I knew everybody's name. And I can tell you their stories. I found out that *everybody had a dream, and everybody had a hurt*. Here were these two beautiful girls; their brother was murdered some years ago. But they knew they'd find an even more beautiful faith than they already had when they went back to the Holy Land, and they did. Here was another woman, a lovely woman. Her husband had died many years ago, leaving her with little children. Everybody has a hurt. Everybody has a dream. Everybody needs to be loved. And I've never been happier than I was on that tour because there were eighty people that I was able to know and meet and love. That's a great, great feeling, it really is!

Love. You need it. I need it. Everybody, all over the world, needs it.

I remember two years ago this summer I was in Russia. Russia, as you know, has tried to educate man into being a cold, calculating, intellectualized, rationalized creature, so that he's basically a computer that responds to the guy who pushes a button. Communism basically says that man, the emotional creature, is weak. It is at this doctrine of man that Communism and Christianity are totally irreconcilable, because Communism says that man is basically a rational creature, and Christianity says that man is basically an emotional creature.

I subscribe to a couple of wire services, and here's what came over the wire service only a few weeks ago. Listen to it:

"Communist China has denounced the Kremlin leaders for allowing religious fever to grip the Soviet Union. Peking radio, in a recent boadcast, said that a religious fever is spreading across the Communist Soviet Union. Describing what is called 'an upsurge in religious practice in the Soviet Union,' the Chinese broadcast continued, ' . . . tens of thousands of religious believers swarmed into the churches this past Easter. There they ate wafers, they made crosses and sang hymns to celebrate the resurrection of Jesus. Moscow's 54 churches, guarded by police and militant groups, were jammed packed. Why has such a phenomenon of such social retrogression appeared in a so-called developed socialist country, in the land of the great Lenin?' " the broadcast asked rhetorically. Well, we know the answer.

This summer I went through Zurich, and I thought of Solzhenitzyn who is living there now. Solzhenitzyn — *think of it, the number one poet in the Soviet Union* — product of its educational systems, product of its indoctrination, product of its scientfic materialism, product of its dialectical materialism, always protected from Western influences, now has come out and made this statement: "I myself see Chrsitianity as the only living spiritual force capable of healing my land." It's incredible! Even a half-century-old, totally repressive society based on total control is not able to change man's deep heart hunger for love.

What is that love that satisfies? It is only Christ. It is only God. That's what it is!

Now the good news I have, and it applies to every person, no matter who you are, is that God has set things up in such a way that He is able to provide love to your hungry heart. Even though you may think you're a very, very little person, *He knows you*. And He'll take care of your heart's hunger for love.

I had breakfast one morning this summer in a tiny little restaurant in the Bea Rivage Hotel, in Laussane, Switzerland, and talked with Malcolm Muggeridge. You may not know the name, but Malcolm Muggeridge is probably the most recognized face and name in the English empire. A recent poll conducted in London asked, "What face would you recognize first on the street?" Malcolm Muggeride was No. 1; the Queen of England was No. 2. Now that's how famous he is! He's probably in his 60's, I would gather. Some of you know him because he writes a column in a national magazine in America every month. Some of you know him as the Editor of Punch Magazine. He's had an interesting life. As a young man he was a radical socialist. He thought that social-ism, as an economic system, would solve all the human problems and we'd have a perfect society. From that he moved on into agnosticism, and then he became an atheist. Then he was fascinated by communism. So as a journalist he requested an assignment to the Soviet Union and was given it. He spent years there, only to discover to his chagrin that it was a repressive society, that it didn't satisfy; it just didn't have the answers.

A few years ago he was under the assignment of journalism which took him into an encounter in India. In Calcutta he ran across a diminutive little girl (they call her a little girl but she's a woman in her 70's probably) by the name of Mother Theresa, a Roman Catholic nun. Now there are loads of people in this world who are on the edge of sainthood. They're such beautiful Christians, but nobody comes closer to be-ing called a saint and earning it than Mother Theresa. She took the dying people from the streets of Cal-cutta, touched them, loved them and kissed them so that as they were dying they would know that some-body loved them while they were leaving the earth. Incredible!

Well, Muggeridge met her, and he saw a love that you cannot explain by psychology, any science or by any anthropological principles. You cannot explain it from a sociological, a political or economic stand-point. There's only one way to explain it: *Something* has gripped that woman! "It" is Christ. Well, it caused Muggeridge to start reading his Bible. To make a long story short, he's a Chistian today. As he has said, "Hedonism, as a philosophy, can be very appealing for those who can stand it and those who can afford it. After all, the lusts of life can be very, very delightful. The earth's smells and sounds can be very sweet. Sexual love can bring its golden hours, but, in the end, it does not satisfy.

"Still there was something in my heart that was hungry. Now that I look back on it, it is as if I were all my life in a dungeon where both of my hands were manacled, and around me were crowds of people with their manacled hands in the same dungeon. Fantasies and furies were around me. In my fantasies there was no God, no heaven, no hell, no sin and no Saviour. Yes, I felt manacled. One manacle was the desires of my body and flesh and my lust; the other manacle my will and its driving me to do and to be. Then suddenly a couple of years ago I looked up and in my dungeon I saw a light, a window in the top and light coming out. Above it, I suspected, a whole heaven! The heaven was God! The window was Jesus Christ! The ray that shone down on me was the Holy Spirit! And love came to me, love such as I have never known, and it was beautiful."

It can happen to you. If you're in a dungeon and you feel manacled, look up! Find Love!

LOVE . . . it is the greatest!

CHAPTER TWO

I Love Christ
too much
to ever
doubt God!

"Love believes all things."
(I Cor. 13:7)

2

LOVE — The Force that puts Power in your Faith

"Love believes all things."

For years I've read I Corinthians 13 with what I now view to be a distorted impression. I've always thought that Paul was really holding up three lovelies in a beauty contest. One was Faith, one was Hope and one was Love. And when the final contest was completed, Love won the crown, Faith came in second, and Hope was the first runnerup. In other words, I had the impression that Paul was putting Faith and Love and Hope *in competition* with each other. Now that's not a true interpretation at all. The insight I have now, and I'm excited to share it with you, is that what Paul is simply saying is that the three are a Holy Trinity. Love is what wraps them all together. The tuth is, love is a mighty faith-building power. *"Love believes all things."* (I Cor. 13:7.)

So, 1st Corinthians chapter 13 is not a putdown of faith.

You've got to believe, you know. Blake put it this way:

> "Life's dim windows of the soul
> Distort the heavens from pole to pole.
> And makes us to believe a lie
> When we see with and not through the eye."

We need faith. The truth is, *love is impossible without faith, and faith is unacceptable without love.* Think of that: *Love is impossible without faith.*

I've been married for twenty-five years to my first and only wife, and if you ask me what is love, I would say first of all, it is *respect;* secondly, it is *faith.*

I am thinking of a man who is unmarried. He is in his 50's. He was despairing before me recently because his life is lonely; he has never had a family. "The trouble is," he said, "I once knew a young girl, but there wasn't the passion for her that I thought should have been there, so I foolishly thought I didn't love her. However, I deeply respected and trusted her! Now, in retrospect, I see that this was love, but I didn't know it! And I let it pass me by."

Today I call upon you to build your faith around a heart of love. Have you seen people who have faith which seems to move mountains? And other people who profess faith in God and in Jesus Christ, but nothing miraculous or joyful seems to be happening in their lives? Now what's the difference? The difference probably is that the one person has a faith with a heart of love. And the other person has a faith but love is not at the heart of it! That's what Paul is talking about here. So what I'm saying is that love is the power-center behind a mountain-moving faith. When love is at the core of your faith, it puts five miracle-working powers into your belief.

1. *Love puts renewing power in faith.* When love is so strong it won't allow you to doubt for long, then it puts power at the center of your faith. Some people say to me, "Dr. Schuller, where do you get your faith?" And I think the answer is simple: *I love Christ too much to ever doubt God!*

If at the core of your faith there is love — for your work, for your project, for your dream, for your cause, for your husband, for your wife—when love is at the power-core of faith, then faith will never quit. It will come back, it will start over, it will try again. You will reorganize, you will reschedule, you will re-examine, you will rededicate, but you do not resign. The kind of faith that never quits, the kind of faith that is constantly renewed, is faith that has love at the center. Faith and love are twins. Love puts renewing power in faith. Then what happens?

2. *Love puts realigning power in faith.* What do I mean? I mean when love is in the core of your faith, you constantly realign your faith to make sure that your faith is focusing on service and not on yourself. And that's crucial.

I recently had to have my tires realigned. I got new tires four months ago and I haven't put many miles on them, but suddenly I looked at them the other day and I noticed they were completely worn on one side. And what was worse, I could hardly drive down the freeway without almost jiggling apart. It was absolutely uncontrollable to drive. So I had my front wheels realigned.

And you and I must do this with our faith constantly. Realign your faith to make sure that your faith is focused on service and not on yourself.

I recently received a letter from one of the Presbyterian pastors who was here for our last Institute for Successful Church Leadership. In it he wrote, "You know, that Institute changed my life. When I was a young man and had just entered the ministry, I really had my eyes on Christ, and it was beautiful. Somewhere along the line I got my eyes off Him and I became ambitious. My eyes were on professional pursuits and on my career. When Dr. Schuller shared how real Jesus Christ was to him, He became real to me again. My life has been changed." He's been realigned, you see. Love at the power-center of your faith will cause you to refocus on service and not on self. Love at the power-center, then, gives constant renewing power, constant realigning power, and obviously what follows then is that you get restraining power on your faith.

3. *Love puts restraining power on faith*: Power to keep your faith from running over people just to get what you want. Remember, love without faith is impossible; and faith without love is totally unacceptable. It's downright damaging.

A businessman said to me once after I had finished one of my lectures at a sales conference, "I've got a problem. You know, I really think that I could expand my business to really cover the whole country, but if I did it I would put a lot of little guys out of business. As a Christian I don't think I should do that, do you?" I answered, "I don't think so either."

4. *Love puts a redeeming power in faith.* When there is love at the power-center of your faith, there is a renewing power, a realigning power, and a restraining power. Naturally, then, your faith becomes a redeeming power. Instead of hurting people, you help people. Instead of being a destroyer, you become a builder. Instead of just being a teacher, trying to draw your maximum salary and maximum benefits, you're primarily concerned about these kids and how you can build a person. And as a doctor you're not primarily concerned about how many fees you can attract, but can you be a physician who heals the whole person. And as a businessman you're primarily concerned not about profit margins, you must concern yourself with that, but you're constantly concerned about serving people who have needs that must be met. And if you're a lawyer, you look upon

yourself as a counsellor to help people and to advise
them. And if you're a laboring man or delivery man,
you really want to help people. You care about them.

A couple of weeks ago, when we spent a few days
at our mountain cabin, it was necessary for me to
order two deliveries to our place. Both deliveries really shocked me. The first item came in a paper box in
kind of a heavy carton. The man drove his truck up
and put it at the front door. I was going to say goodbye when he said, "It's kind of heavy. Where would
you like it? Can't I carry it in for you?" I said,
"Well, yes, thank you." And so he brought it in the
house. "Be glad to carry it upstairs for you," he continued. I was amazed. Then he cut the carton open,
which kind of shocked me, and said, "Let's make sure
all the pieces are here before I leave. It would be too
bad if I got home and you found a couple of pieces
missing." (I've had that happen. Haven't you?)

He took the thing out, checked all the pieces, and
they were all there. Then he picked up all the pieces
of paper, stuffed them in the box and asked, "Do you
want the box or shall I take it along for you?" I said,
"That would be fine." And then he saw some little
mess that he had made from some of this stuff and
said, "Do you have a broom?" I got out a broom and
a pan and he swept it up. I couldn't believe it. He
looked at me and said, "Haven't I met you some
place? You sure look familiar." "Do you ever watch
religious television programs?" I asked. His face
glowed as he answered, "Oh, you're Dr. Schuller. I
didn't recognize you in your swimming suit!" He
then really opened up. "Isn't this business of being

a Christian wonderful?" He was full of the Spirit of Christ. And I said, "It sure makes a difference in people, when it turns you into the kind of delivery-man you are. That's great."

Now, then, only a few days after that I had another delivery, and it was the same kind of story. The guy couldn't do enough to be helpful. And when he left he thought he recognized me. Then he told me, "Oh, we've enjoyed the Hour of Power. In fact, I'm a committed Christian, and I'm going to be a minister. I just don't have enough education yet to have a church of my own. But I'm going to go into full-time ministry of the Lord, and thank you for what you've done in my life."

Faith is constantly *renewed* if love is at the core. Faith is constantly *realigned* if love is at the core. Faith is constantly *restrained* if love is at the core. Faith is constantly *redeemed* if love is at the core. No wonder, then, that faith is constantly *rejoicing* if love is at the core. And that's what makes faith a mountain-moving power, because the rejoicing keeps you so energetic, so joyful, so happy.

5. *Love puts rejoicing power in your faith.* What good is faith if it will die, or if it's damaging, or if it leads to despair? Your faith does not need to be that way. It can rejoice!

We all know people who have a lot of positive thinking and possibility thinking. They make their goals, they achieve success, they even become very wealthy and sometimes very powerful and end up dying from an overdose. What good is that?

Love without faith is impossible, and faith without love is totally unacceptable. All the possibility thinking in the world is dangerous unless Jesus Christ, through the Holy Spirit, has control over your heart and fills you with His love. If that happens, you will be happy in your success because you will be so helpful.

I was preaching in New Jersey this summer, and there was a line of people who met me afterwards. In the line was one young man who said, "I'm a Presbyterian pastor, and I made this trip which took me a couple of hundred miles to drive here to meet you, Dr. Schuller. I'm so glad you agreed to meet people afterwards, because I've come bearing a message. One of the leading members of my church, who was in her late 40's, died sometime ago from cancer. The last year she was unable to come out to church at all. Every Sunday she watched television, the Hour of Power, in her New Jersey bedroom. Shortly before she passed away she said to me, 'Reverend, if you ever get a chance to meet anybody from that Hour of Power or Dr. Schuller, please go and bring him this message from me. Tell him that because of his ministry, *I didn't spend the last year of my life dying from cancer, I spent the last year of my life living with cancer.*' "

Do you see why I'm happy? When Christ is in the center of your life, then love is at the center of your faith! Your faith is constantly renewed; it does not die. It's constantly realigned; it's not distracted. It's constantly restrained, never demeaning.

It's constantly redeeming, never destructive. So it's constantly rejoicing, never despairing.

Chapter Three

No man has a right to demand all of his rights all of the time!

"Love seeketh not her own."
(I Cor. 13:5)

3

Compromise Can Be Kingly

"Love seeketh not her own."

One of the revised versions translates that phrase this way:

"Love does not demand its own way."

I suggest that this brings us to the thought that compromise can be kingly. We all have been warned from childhood never to compromise. And indeed it is a truth that there are principles that you must never compromise. Remember Tovyeh, the father hero in "Fiddler on the Roof?" He had that surprisingly marvelous balance in the realm of compromising. He had the ability to see both sides when he said, " . . . on the other hand . . . " But he reaches one point when he says, "There is no other hand!" There is a point beyond which you cannot compromise.

All of which leads us to probably one of the most important questions we have to ask as Christians, and that is, "When do we compromise and when don't we?"

Have you noticed that love, for some people, is very wishie-washie, while love, for others, seems to be strong as steel? The people whose love is strong as steel are people for whom self-denial is at the core of their love. For what is compromising? It is self-denial. Compromising is lowering yourself only to be lifted.

Two boys were trying to play on a hobby horse outside of a department store where you put in a dime and the horse goes up and down. They were both trying to ride at the same time when one boy said, "You know, if both of us didn't try to get on at the same time, I could have a much better ride."

Compromising is lowering yourself to give *someone else an opportunity.*

Compromising is looking; looking for better ideas, new insights, broader views, brighter ways to help. It assumes that somebody else knows something you don't know.

Compromising is listening: It's listening to what others are saying. It's listening to what others are demanding. It's listening to what others claim are their rights. It's listening to what others hold as their opinions, their views and their interpretations of the Bible, even when you don't agree.

We've reached a point in our world and in our country where without compromising we're all going to be bruised over the same hobby horse, and nobody is going to have a decent ride.

Compromising is looking, listening, lowering and *living with the spirit of community.* A give-and-take attitude. If you forget everything else I say in this message, don't forget this next sentence:

NO MAN HAS A RIGHT TO DEMAND ALL OF HIS RIGHTS ALL OF THE TIME

"I know my rights," you say. No man has a right to demand all of his rights all of the time, if he wants to be a part of a community. So what's compromising? It's looking for better ideas, broader views. It's listening to what others are saying, thinking and interpreting. And it's living with them, even when you don't share their viewpoint.

Compromising is learning how to live abundantly, even when you don't get your way. And it's learning how to be happy and pleasant, instead of being a baby and pouting just because things don't go the way you want them to go. That's what compromise is. It's looking, it's listening, it's living, it's learning, and it's summed up in two words: *Letting go!*

Yes, *compromising is letting God have His way and His will in your life.* That probably will be what you really do not want to do! But that's the difference between being moral or immoral. An immoral person is somebody who does what he wants to do, when he wants to do it, the way he wants to do it, whether it is right or not. That's immorality. By contrast, morality is doing what is right, even if you don't like it.

Compromise can be kingly then, can't it?! When you look for better ideas, when you listen to what others are saying and thinking, when you live with the spirit of community and begin to learn how to live happily even when your man isn't elected to office, and when you learn then to let go and lower yourself and let God take over, can't you see this is when compromise is kingly?

So when do you compromise? That's the question. I want to suggest four times when compromising will make a peasant into a king:

1. *Compromise in the face of a hurt that you can do nothing about.*

I had a telephone call recently from my friend, Pat Shaughnessy. Pat Shaughnessy is the pastor of a church in Phoenix, Arizona. His church was not moving and he wasn't able to come to the Institute at the time it was in session, so he got a copy of my book, "Move Ahead with Possibility Thinking." As he's told many people, it transformed his life and it transformed his church which is suddenly blossoming and growing. Right now they're building a million dollar church to handle the bulging congregation.

I tell him, "God spoke to you through the book, Pat, and I thank Him for that. I prayed for that. Give credit where credit is due. It's God who did it." "Yes, you're right," he said.

When I returned from Europe recently there was a memo for me to call Pat at a Los Angeles hospital. "What are you doing there?" I asked. And he said, "Let me tell you what happened. I was on my way to Korea a few weeks ago, standing at the Pan Am air counter, when all of a sudden there was an explosion. Three people were killed. I was closest to the bomb, and suddenly I found myself lying on the floor. My right leg was blown off between the hip and the knee. Blood just gushed out. But I never lost consciousness. My first thought was, 'Lord, if I have to go, I'm ready. But I don't want to. I enjoy preaching about Jesus so much because Christ is such a wonderful person.' My second thought was, 'My wife, I hoped that she would not be too hurt by what is happening to me.' Then on the way to the hospital they were pumping blood into me, and it was a mad scene. They said I wouldn't live, and I was wide awake. Then this thought struck me, 'I don't need a right leg to preach the gospel!'"

Pat has compromised. He has accepted the loss of a leg. Look at what you have left, not at what you have lost. You must compromise in the face of a hurt or a loss that you cannot change.

2. *Compromise in the face of humility.*

I recall an incident in the life of Schweitzer, that great dedicated man who had over fifty honorary doctorate degrees. Albert Schweitzer has to be one of the greatest men of our century. He built his hospital in Africa, in the Belgian Congo. The natives normally would do anything for him. But one day when he needed wood hauled to build a wall, he asked one tribal native to carry some wood. The native, who had learned to read and was busy reading a book, said, "I am an intellectual and I do not carry wood." Schweitzer, in the face of that, looked at him and said, "Well, I congratulate you. I always wanted to be an intellectual, but I never succeeded, so I'll carry the wood." And he did!

3. *Compromise in the face of helpfulness.*

I recall an incident in the life of Abraham Lincoln. At the height of the Civil War, he wondered how the battle was going. Rather than call General Mc-Clellan to come to him at the White House and report, he decided that he and the Secretary of War would go out to the General's house in the battle area. They made their way to the General's home and waited. Finally the General came in, walked right on upstairs to his room and never acknowledged the President. They thought he'd be back in a minute with cleaner garb, but he didn't come back. They asked the maid to go upstairs, but when she came down she was aghast! "I'm sorry, Mr. President," she said, "but he said to me, 'Tell the President I'm tired and that I've gone to bed.'" The Secretary of War said, "Surely you're not going to let him get by with that. You will relieve him, will you not?" The President thought about it for a long time, and finally when he broke the silence he said, "No, I will not relieve him. That man wins battles, and I would hold his horse and clean his shoes if it would hasten the end of this bloodshed by one hour."

Doesn't that remind you of our Lord Jesus Christ? He overheard His followers talking behind his back. "When Jesus is gone, who is going to be the top man here? You, Peter, you, John, or Luke?" Do you know what Jesus did? He asked for a basin of water and He asked for a towel. And before they had their communion He got down and started to wash their feet. Peter said, "Wait a minute, I should wash your feet. You shouldn't wash mine." But He just moved from foot to foot and washed their dirty feet and wiped them with a towel.

You compromise if you can teach somebody a lesson by doing it, indeed you do. Schweitzer hauled wood. Lincoln would hold the man's horse. Jesus washed the disciples' feet. Great men have become kings by learning when to bow, when to compromise.

4. *Compromise in the face of holiness.*

Don't you sense it, that there is a God and that He has a plan for your life? Don't you feel it? That there's a road that He wants you to walk on? Some of you are running so fast. But, what's the use of running so fast if you're on the wrong road? I would add, I see what some of you people are holding on to in life. For some it may be status, for others dollars, and others things. All of which some day will have to slip out of your hand. And when your life is finished they will mean nothing to you. I would ask you this question, *"What's the use of holding on to something that isn't tied down to anything?"*

Once God came to this world in the form of a man, and He died on the cross to prove to you that He loves you so much that He would stop at nothing to save you. And to gain power out of that cross, even eternal life, you must compromise your will to God's will. Say, "Father, not my will but Thine be done." *There is no conversion without compromise!*

You know, in old England when someone was to be knighted, the queen or the king tapped each shoulder of that person with a sword, and he was declared to be a knight. But there's one thing they had to do in order to become a knight. They had to be humble; they had to kneel; they had to bow; they had to compromise their pride. *They had to kneel to be knighted.*

I invite you now, whoever you are, to compromise what probably for you may be your pride, your greed, or maybe it's stubbornness, self-pity, jealousy, bitterness or your lust for something that is a sin that will keep God's Holy Spirit out of your life.

I suggest that you remember these words: *"Love does not demand its own way."* Love knows when you should give in and give up.

Let go and let God take over!

CHAPTER FOUR

A *beautiful*
person is always
a successful person.
And any person
can be beautiful!
So anyone
can live beyond failure.

"Love never fails."
(I Cor. 13:8)

4

Living Beyond the Possibility
of Personal Failure

"Love never fails."

My text now is from verse 8 of I Corinthians, Chapter 13, *"Love never fails."* I would say, *you can love and lose, but you cannot love and fail.* You can love and lose your life, (as happened to Jesus Christ on the cross), but you cannot fail as a person when you really love people sincerely.

Every human being can live beyond the possibility of personal failure. Everyone can be a success if he can learn to love. And that's all-important! For I don't suppose anything is more important than the consciousness that you, as a person, are a success and not a failure.

I remember so vividly a telephone call I received. It was from a woman calling from the midwest. She said, "Dr. Schuller, I am in my mid-50's, and I'm finished with life." I told her that was a very negative attitude, but she continued, "But you don't know my life. I was a failure in high school. And I failed to go to college. I was a failure in my first marriage. My kids haven't turned out right, and I feel I'm a failure as a mother. I'm a failure as a wife. I never had a good job. My life has been one big fat failure. I'm not going to keep going." And I'll tell you, my eyes were moist. How do you keep from crying when you come right down to a heart that is cracked and broken?

Nothing is more damning to the human spirit and to your mental health than if you ever get the idea that you have been a big failure. Success is a necessity.

W. Somerset Maugham said, "There's a common idea that success spoils people by making them vain and egotistical, but the truth is, this is erroneous and on the contrary, it makes people, for the most part, humble and tolerant and gentle. It is failure that makes people bitter and cruel. You need to feel that you are successful."

A few weeks ago I read an article by Dr. Bertram Brown, the Director of the National Institute for Mental Health. In it he discussed a major problem in our country today, depression, and he listed this phenomenal statistic: Mental depression costs the United States $5 billion a year; that's in direct hospital-drugs expense which does not include the indirect cost of depression in forms of the funerals of the suicide victims. This does not include the expense to the taxpayers of people who are in mental hospitals, supported by your taxes, because they are depressed. The *direct,* immediate expense is $5 billion a year! Dr. Brown said, "Suicide today is the third cause of death among teenagers and the eleventh cause among Americans in general."

Then Dr. Brown was asked the question, "Is there anything a depressive person can do for himself, short of seeking psychiatric help?" The doctor's answer was, "Yes. Build into yourself the idea that you are not helpless and you are not hopeless." [1] Then the question was addressed to him, "But how can you build into a person the feeling that he is not helpless and his life is not hopeless?" He answered, "Give them success experiences to counteract feelings of helplessness." That's where it comes out, and I hope that in some small measure what I say here will help to give you the key to success so that you will not feel helpless in the face of life and so that you will not feel you are a failure and become a part of the millions of Americans who are down and depressed.

[1] U.S. News & World Report, Sept. 9, 1974 (pg. 38)

I can assure you without any hesitation, without any exception, everyone can be a success. This is what I mean: You can succeed as a person, even if you do not succeed professionally. We must have a definition, of course, of *success*. By success we do not mean that you have a multimillion dollar income. We are not measuring success now, in terms of dollars, status, fame or fortune.

Many years ago, when Dr. Beckering was a pastor in Chicago, Illinois, he was asked to make a call on the husband of one of the wives of his congregation. This man, who was sick in his hospital bed, turned out to be a great nationally known physician in his own right. Dr. Beckering thought to himself, "What can I say to this great doctor, who now is on his bed with a near-fatal heart attack?" When Dr. Beckering went into the room, the patient saw him and said, "Dr. Beckering, I'm glad to see you. Since I've been a patient myself here, I've had a revelation. The revelation, Dr. Beckering, is that *it is not what you do in life that counts, it is what you are.* I've done a lot, but I'm not the person I should have been." *It's not what you do, but what you are!* He became, and is today, a fantastic Christian!

Which reminds me of what Goethe said, "Before you can do something, you have to be somebody." That means you have to *be* a beautiful person before you can do anything beautiful.

It's not what you do, it's what you are that counts. In that light, we can define *success*: *A beautiful person is a successful person, so beautiful people are never failures.* They may lose, but they do not fail. You can love and lose, but you cannot love and fail, for when you love you are beautiful.

I did some research recently on some of the great capitalists who made America great. I got interested because of the problem of inflation that we have in our country. So I did some research, and I found that Andrew Carnegie, who in his lifetime made a half billion dollars, made a profound statement. He said, "It's impossible to get rich without doing a lot of good for a lot of people." Now that was his attitude! Do you know what his goal was? Carnegie's goal was to bring the price of steel down from $160 a ton to $20 a ton, and he did it!

I also did some research on Henry Ford. Do you know what his burning desire was? His burning desire was to produce an automobile and do it good enough and cheap enough so that every American family could afford an automobile in their garage.

I studied a man named Gillette. He wanted to make it possible for every man to have a clean shave *cheap!*

And there was a man named Ingersoll who liked watches. When he was a young man he couldn't afford one. His goal was to produce watches for $1 so every man could have a watch in his pocket.

The greatest capitalists in American history made millions because their attitudes were not to make millions but to do a lot of good for a lot of common people. And with that attitude capitalism came very close to achieving the goal that socialists have proposed, namely, abundance for all in a classless society.

And now inflation threatens our country, and do you know why? I'm going to suggest something. Inflation is threatening the very life of capitalism because the *attitude* has changed in too many corporations (both in labor and in management) to "How can we get the most for ourselves," instead of "How can we do the most good for the most people." If that attitude dominates for long then capitalism will die, because everybody will try to get all they can for themselves; that will feed inflation which can kill our system.

So how do you change people's attitudes? By getting love inside! When you get a love for people as *persons,* (when I'm focused on service and not on self), you produce success.

Carnegie was right. Nobody is going to get rich and keep his riches unless he does a lot of good for a lot of people.

Love never fails, but selfishness always, ultimately is suicidal. Get love inside, and you will be a successful person.

I said to an old woman, who was over 70 and under 100, "You are so beautiful." She looked at me and said, "Well, I ought to be. I've lived with Him," and her eyes looked up to her Lord, "for 80 years."

Love never fails to produce successful, beautiful people.

Archibald Rutledge tells of a captain of one of the ships on the Mississippi River. One day the captain went to the engine room which was always spotlessly clean. As you know, engine rooms are usually the greasiest, dirtiest places on a ship. The captain said to the engineer, "Why is your engine room always so clean?" And the man said, "Well, Captain, it's like this: I got a glory inside of me!"

Once there was a man who came onto these grounds, about two years ago, stubbled beard, drunk, an outcast, and the law came looking for him and caught him. They put him in jail. From his cell, a half mile east, he could see the cross on top of our Tower of Hope. He made contact with the lay people of this church, and they loved him and told him he could be saved, he could be born again, he could be literally transformed, changed, made into a different, new human being. And he believed it, and he accepted Jesus Christ.

What a conversion! So our church vouched for him. We gave him a job to clean up the place. He not only cleaned up the place, he went out and bought some paint and painted our engine room. You should see it! Every pipe is painted, every nut is painted, every washer is painted, every cable is painted, every engine is painted, every motor is painted, and the ceiling is painted blue with white stars. Purple, red, green, blue, orange, lavender, pink — you can't imagine how such a conglomeration of every color in the rainbow and a dozen more can be put into that one room, and it looks gorgeous! It's absolutely the most beautiful engine room in any place in the world! I said to him, "Why did you paint it this way?" "Because," he said, "that's the way I feel inside, since Jesus Christ came in."

You can live beyond the possibility of failure by becoming a beautiful person. You can become a beautiful person by taking Christ into your life. When that happens, LOVE will dominate your personality. And love never fails! So any person can be a great success personally if he'll simply turn his life over to Jesus Christ.

So my question is not how many dollars you have, not how much status you have, not how famous you are nor what position you have. My question is, Do you have Jesus Christ in your life?

CHAPTER FIVE

I offer to you Jesus Christ. Take Him and you'll have an end to loneliness.

*"So faith, hope, love abide, these three;
but the greatest of these is love."*

(I Cor. 13:13)

5

Here's a Love to End Your Loneliness

"So faith, hope, love abide, these three;
but the greatest of these is love."

I have for you an answer to what is undoubtedly one of the biggest problems in the world today, and that is the problem of *loneliness.*

Standing in my pulpit recently, addressing a full church, was a friend of mine who watches Hour of

Power from her home in Minneapolis, Minnesota. Many of you know her as Dear Abby, a columnist whose column appears in over 900 newspapers. She said to me, "Dr. Schuller, loneliness, and the need for love that goes with it, is the number one problem that faces people." She told me she receives over 10,000 letters a week, and we receive that many ourselves. We both agreed that it is man's hunger for acceptance and understanding that is, of all needs, deepest.

Here is God's answer to the problem of loneliness:

"So faith, hope, love abide, these three; but the greatest of these is love." (I Cor. 13:13)

Why is love greater than anything else? Because love alone meets man's deepest need, woman's deepest need and a child's deepest need, and that need is to be accepted where I am, as I am.

Loneliness is a battle that takes place between two persons who live inside of you within your soul. No person is so integrated that he is only one self. But deep within us there are many conflicting persons. Life is a crew of people within us, struggling to take over the helm.

Look at these two people within you: There is one person reaching out for love, like a little child in a candy store grasping for candy. This person reaches out desperately, anxiously, almost hysterically for love and understanding. But there is another self who, like a father holding back a child's hand in a candy store, says to your grabbing self, "Look out! Don't grab so fast. You might get hurt. You might be re-

jected. You might not be accepted. You don't want
to love and be rejected, do you? Love is a risky business, you know. To love is to be vulnerable. To be
vulnerable is to be accountable. To be accountable
is to run the risk of being rejected. To be rejected
you run the risk of all risks, and that is that you
might end up hating yourself because others don't
love you."

And so the lonely person is the one who listens ultimately to fear instead of to faith. The lonely person
is somebody who listens finally to the self that says,
"Be careful. Don't take any chances. Don't make any
commitments. Don't get involved. You might get
rejected. You might get hurt." And if that's the voice
you listen to, you will have your freedom intact, but
the price you pay for your freedom from involve-
ment is loneliness. One reason our society is so infect-
ed with loneliness is because the spirit of selfish freedom has become so widespread. So we don't want to
risk losing our freedom by getting involved. We don't
want to lose our freedom by running the risks of
making long-term commitments. So there are those
who say, "What's the use of marriage? It's only a
piece of paper. Live together, love together." And
if the relationship cools you can split, you can go
your way, and nobody will get hurt. The fallacy of
that is that the man loves the girl only as long as she's
young. And then when the wrinkles come, he deserts
her. And when she's old, nobody cares, because she
sold herself too cheaply.

We have a lot of lonely people today because the

price of unwillingness to make permanent commitments is to live on a level of interpersonal relationships where all relationships are temporary. When you are hurt, like infantile children who pack up their marbles, you can go your way and find yourself free again. But remember, one day you may land in the hospital for major surgery and discover that nobody knows, and nobody cares! Unless you are willing to surrender some freedom to make permanent commitments, prepare to pay the price, *loneliness.*

Love ends loneliness, but love has a price tag. The price tag of love is commitment to continuity. Like I said to a young couple the other day, "What makes marriage more important than a piece of paper? *One thing,* and that is when you say, 'I love you and always will love you, even when your skin is wrinkled.' That's when you're going to need it more than ever."

There are all kinds and forms of loneliness. "The Loneliness of Sinking," "The Loneliness of Suffering," "The Loneliness of Struggling," "The Loneliness of Striving," "The Loneliness of Searching," "The Loneliness of Succeeding," and finally, "The Loneliness of Sinning." Where do you fit in? Let's look at some of them briefly:

1. *The Loneliness of Sinking.* Failure, of course, brings its own loneliness. Because when things aren't going right and you're facing bankruptcy, or your marriage is falling apart, and you have that sinking, failing feeling, you have a loneliness because you don't want to share your failure with others. You'd rather not talk about your failures! Nobody wants to hear

a loser cry. (Except — it strikes me all of a sudden — that's one thing that is unique about Jesus Christ: He always has time to listen to a loser cry!)

2. *The Loneliness of Succeeding.* I don't know which is the worst. I have known the Loneliness of Sinking. There were two years in this ministry when the will to die was stronger than the will to live. I had dreams of a church with fountains and grounds where people could worship in their cars and inside the sanctuary. I had the whole vision. God showed me a tower with 24-hour telephone counselling and a staff of great ministers and a thousand more lay people like you who would do Christ's work. The whole dream was there. And the problems were momentous. I was sure I was failing. I know the Loneliness of Sinking. And I've known the Loneliness of Succeeding. For when you succeed, who wants to listen to you? With whom do you dare share your victories? Most people will think you're boasting! So there is the Loneliness of Success as well as the Loneliness of Sinking.

3. The *Loneliness of Struggling.* This is the time when you don't know if you're sinking or succeeding. You only know you're struggling! And you don't want to publicly admit you have problems. You don't want to show weakness; you don't want to expose imperfection. You want to hopefully keep a strong front.

You might remember hearing somewhere years ago someone utter a ghastly negative sentence that said,

"Even rats flee from sinking ships." So you don't want to expose the fact that you've got problems. Well, the truth is, every person in this world has problems. As Dr. Peale said in this pulpit one day, "Everybody has problems. The only person who doesn't have problems is dead. Anybody who is alive, really alive, has problems." Of course I would add: Anyone who is alive is getting involved. And a person who is getting involved is taking risks. And a person who is taking risks is living on the edge of nerve; he's taking a chance, and that's what makes him alive instead of dead with boredom.

4. *The Loneliness of Striving.* What do you do when you strive? God gives you a dream. Do you dare to tell people? It takes a lot of courage to love. It doesn't take much courage to hate, but it takes a lot of courage to love. There is the fear of what people will say, especially if we think big. Will they laugh and say, "Who do you think you are that you can be that person? Who do you think you are that you could amount to something? Boy, has something gone to your head! Wow, are you an egomaniac!" The fear of ridicule drives us to isolation which results in the Loneliness of Striving.

There is not infrequently an understandable fear that your ideas and your plans might be stolen by someone else. And you have to be protective of your concepts, until at least you have an option or a copyright or a patent. Meanwhile there's the Loneliness of Striving and Struggling and Succeeding and Sinking.

5. *The Loneliness of Searching.* Who has not known this Searching between the choices: Searching for the alternatives; Searching until you make the decision. Ultimately you alone make most of the decisions in your life. Ultimately you live alone. Peripheral living is corporate living, but solitary living is ultimate living. Let me explain.

For the most part, most of us live in interpersonal relationships; acting, reacting, responding, answering to the questions and the challenges and the instincts and the impulses of people around us. But that's peripheral living. Peripheral living is collective (or corporate) living. But ultimate living is solitary living. By that I mean that the ultimate life you live, you live alone. You were born alone. Maybe you had a twin, but both of you were born individually. You were born alone. When you learned to walk, you learned to walk alone. When you learned to talk, you learned to talk alone. True, there were those who guided, supported and sustained you. But you did it alone!

When you make the great decisions, (1) Your career or profession; (2) Whom you will marry, only *you* make these decisions! Nobody else makes the decision. Your father doesn't make it, your mother doesn't make it, your brother or sister don't make it. You do! And ultimately when you accept or reject Jesus Christ, you make that decision. I do not make it for you. Your wife or your husband do not make it for you. Your father or mother do not make it for you. Your pastor or your church do not make it for you. You cannot cop out. You, and you alone, make that decision.

Peripheral living is corporate living, but ultimate living is solitary living.

And finally there comes the time when you die, and that is a moment alone. There will be those who will stand around you. They may be supportive and they may be helpful. But you go alone. All alone. Unless, unless you have a very special friend.

Dr. Glasser, whose book, "Reality Therapy," has been helpful to many people, has a sentence that I find very, very significant. He says, "Every man needs one essential friend." I would add: If you've got that, then you've got a cure for loneliness. And what do we mean? We mean that every person should have one friend who is so intimate that he can expose himself completely to him without making himself vulnerable, without fear that someday he'll tell or he'll be exposed. Where can you find a friend you can trust like that? I have such a friend. His name is Jesus Christ. He is that one essential friend. I can go to Him and confess all my sins, of thought, word and deed, and know that He will put His arm around my shoulder and love me anyway. I can go to Him in the Loneliness of Striving and He won't put me down. I can go to Him in the Loneliness of Searching for alternatives and ask His advice! I can go to Him in the Loneliness of Struggling and Sinking and be encouraged. I can go to Him in the Loneliness of Succeeding and He will sense my joy. He is the one essential friend who really cures loneliness, for He offers a love that is deep and true and beautiful and lasting, and it never lets you down.

We have beautiful flowers on these grounds. The other day I stopped, for the first time, at the place where we buy these flowers. There I met one of the most remarkable people in my life. She's an old lady. When I went into the shop I saw her sitting behind the counter. She had her wrinkled old elbows on the glass. Her whole face was so wrinkled. Her hair was silver, and it was done with little hand curls in a very homey way. She had glasses on, perched at the tip of her old nose. I went to the desk and she immediately said, "Oh, I want to tell you how much I enjoy you on television. I have some friends who go to a Bible church, and they say, 'Dr. Schuller doesn't preach Bible. He just preaches possibility thinking.' " And she shook a bony finger at the imaginary friend. "But I say to them, 'There's possibility thinking in Scripture.' "

"God bless you," I told her. "Yes, it's Scripture," she continued. "Oh, it's done wonders for me. We came out here from Kansas, my husband and I. Then my husband passed away." "I suppose you're lonely," I commented. She jolted to attention and stood upright. "Lonely? I don't get lonely around here. *There's always a new flower blooming every day.*" She went on, "When the first cyclamen blooms they come running in here and bring it to me! Isn't it pretty?" She was so excited. "Loneliness," she said, "what is it? What is it?" "You're a Christian, aren't you?" I asked. "Oh, yes," she said. "I sure am, Dr.

Schuller. I was converted in a little country church in Kansas when I was a young girl. I can show you the very spot and the very pew where I was saved. And Jesus has been my friend ever since." I looked at her face. It was beautiful for all her wrinkles were happy wrinkles. There wasn't one wrinkle that wasn't carved from a smile or from laughter.

She reminded me of my dad who passed away some years ago at the age of 83. I never knew my dad to experience loneliness. That man had the enormous capability of enjoying solitude without ever getting lonely. He knew how to live in those ultimate moments of solitary isolation with strength, peace of mind, calmness and joy. And I learned more from him than I could ever share with you. As I look back on it, it was because he too had one essential friend.

My dad was a poor man all his life on our Iowa farm, but he kept very busy. When he didn't work the fields, he was usually pounding and hammering in his woodshed or his toolshed. He had an old forge, an old anvil and a heavy hammer. Many times in his spare moments I would hear the ringing of the hammer echoing from the anvil. As a little boy I would run to the toolshed, and there would be the forge, red hot, and in it a red hot piece of iron. He would take it out, red and white hot, lay it on the anvil and crash down the heavy hammer, making an iron frame to hold a pot of blooming geraniums beside the house or a spare part to repair a broken piece of machinery.

But there was more than one time when the hammer was silent as I approached his place of work.

I could hear my dad talking softly to his Friend, his God. Yes, so much like the old man in "Fiddler on the Roof." I would hear him say, "I sure got myself a good-sized mortgage on this place. And we've got to work it out, don't we?"

You will never get lonely as long as there is one person who loves you with a love so great that you know you don't have to be a phoney around Him. You don't have to play games. You don't have to wear a mask. You don't have to pretend. He loves you anyway.

He will never condemn you. He will never scold you. He will never belittle you.

And the price? There is one price He demands — that you make a commitment to love Him forever. Yes, forever. That's the best deal you could ever have, because you will *want* Him forever.

> "What a friend we have in Jesus,
>   All our sins and griefs to bear.
>   What a privilege to carry
>   Everything to Him in prayer."

I offer to you Jesus Christ. Take Him and you'll have a love to end all loneliness.

CHAPTER SIX

Resentments are snowdrifts and forgiveness is the snowplow.

"Love is not resentful."
(I Cor. 13:5)

6

"I Forgive You"
The Language of Love

"Love is not resentful."

Are you carrying resentments? How many fears, how many anxieties, how many worries are you suffering from because you will not forgive somebody who hurt you deeply? How many sunny days are turned grey by your angry mind, seething, quarrelling in fantasy bouts with your adversary, an ex-husband, an ex-wife, a relative, a neighbor, a customer, a client or a clerk? Are you suffering from ulcers or arthritis or high blood pressure or even heart problems because you will not forgive? And how many people are developing wrinkles in their skin that will become permanent creases, monuments to the fact that they spent most of their lives thinking angry thoughts, until the frown wrinkles work their way irreducibly into their countenance? How many friends did you once have who now no longer talk to you because you developed a reputation of pouting, grumbling and complaining because you just couldn't handle the daily resentments that got under your skin?

Which leads me to the verse I want to share with you in the chapters that I'm writing on I Corinthians 13, the great Love chapter. I want to focus now on the words:

"Love is not resentful."
(I Cor. 13:5)

Born and raised in Northwest Iowa, I can recall the first snow. It was wonderful. But what we didn't appreciate were the blizzards, because the blizzards would come in driving winds of 50 to 60 miles an hour until sometimes they closed the road with an impassable drift. We wouldn't be able to get out to the store to buy our food. It was serious. One positive thing was I wouldn't have to go to school! And then I remember we would look out of our farm house half mile down the road to the hill where we could see the snowplow coming, cutting through the drifts, slicing the snow, chopping it up and blowing it into a huge, spewing stream into a ditch. And when the snowplow came through, the road was open again, and we could go for our food. And I could go for my education.

Resentments are snowdrifts, and forgiveness is the snowplow. You see, forgiveness in the eyes of the non-Christian is simply a matter of passive acquittal. But in the Christian context that's not it at all. In the Christian context forgiveness is the snowplow. It means opening the road, removing the barrier, so that you can now communicate and listen again to what people are trying to say. We dialogue and interchange; we move back and forth. Whether it's between my God and myself or a person and myself, forgiveness is a snowplow, not just an eraser on a blackboard.

There are a lot of resentments that build up in lives in a period of a day. And the only way to put joy on your face is to find an overpowering love that can remove them and fill you with forgiveness. "I forgive you," is the language of love.

Now, in order to conquer resentments, in order to submit to the forgiving spirit, let's understand what some of the obstacles are:

Obstacle #1: An extreme sense of justice. I have had a problem with this myself. I have a strong sense of justice. It seems to me that we have to remember what the word of God tells us: *"Vengeance is mine."* (Deut. 32:35)

I have often been helped by the story of Joseph. He was sold by his brothers as a slave to Egypt. They had hoped they could kill him and get him out of the way. He became, however, a ruler. They meant to kill him, and they ended up in the providence of God crowning him. As Joseph said, "You meant it for evil, but God meant it for good." Let justice be handled by the Lord. He knows how to take care of people.

There was a man who was the victim of injustice who said to his pastor, "But wouldn't it be man-like of me to be angry?" And his pastor said, "Indeed it would. But it would be Christ-like of you to forgive."

Obstacle #2: Making a mountain out of a mole-hill. We tend, you know, to emphasize the little negative things that get under our skin and forget all positive qualities. The person who has hurt you, no matter who he is, does have many fine qualities, but chances are, you can't see them.

Once, to illustrate this point, I took before a class (I was teaching in Possibility Thinking) a sheet of paper, 8½ x 11. I tacked it on a board, and with a felt pen I made a circle and a straight line on it. Then I asked members of my class to come up and tell me what they saw. One person said a line; another said a circle. Every person came up, and when the class was finished I said, "Not one of you said, 'I see a sheet of paper.'" The bulk of what I had tacked up was one big sheet of white paper. All they saw were the black spots, but they didn't see the mass of white.

We tend, by nature, to be negative thinkers. We see the wrong, and we don't see the good. That becomes an obstacle. We take a little detail and get hung up on it.

It's like an artist who was teaching his students how to paint. He took them out to paint a sunset. They set up their easels, and began to paint. Just as the sky was reaching its height of colorful glory, they noticed one student who was lost in painting the shingles on a barn in the foreground of the pastoral scene. The teacher said, "Look, if you spend so much time painting the shingles, you will miss the sunset." Don't get so hung up on details that you miss the big picture.

Obstacle #3: *Seeing the possibilities in the offensive experience.* In other words, we forget all of the positive possibilities that are in an offensive situation. We forget that this, too, is the time when you can turn your scars into stars.

A few months ago I was on the East Coast in a very prominent city to deliver a sermon in a huge church on a Sunday morning. I had just come from an international trip only a few hours before. At the Geneva airport I had cashed my two $50 traveler's checks and received two $50 bills in exchange. So, I found myself on a Saturday night staying in a hotel preparing for my sermon for the next morning when I noticed that a particular movie was playing in the neighborhood theatre. A movie I had reason to believe might give me some good sermon illustrations. So Mrs. Schuller and I went to the theatre. We stood in line, a long line, and we could see that the movie was starting in two minutes and I didn't want to miss the opening. Just two minutes before the opening I was at the theatre window. I gave them a $50 bill, and the ticket teller looked at it and said, "I'm sorry, we don't take $50 bills." I said, "You can't reject it. Do you know what that bill says? It says, 'This is legal tender for all debts public and private.' You can't refuse it." (I had my tickets already.) But she said, "I'm sorry, we can't take it."

Now, never in my life have I been a public protester, but the line was getting longer and longer behind me and it was starting to drizzle. I said, "I'm sure you'll take it, because it's a good $50 bill." She said, "I'm sorry, we won't take it." The line got longer, and I was getting impatient. Finally she said, "You've got your tickets." "Alright," I said, "thank you," and I walked in. Then she stuck her neck out and yelled at the head usher, "That man didn't pay!" It happened to be in an area where I have a vast listening audience, and I thought, "Oh God, I hope nobody recognizes me." The usher stopped me and asked, "What's the big idea?" I told him, "She wouldn't take my $50 bill, and it's all I've got. I just left Geneva twelve hours ago, and I'm sorry. But you watch where I sit, and you just check with the hotel and see if there isn't a Robert Schuller listed there, and check out if they think he's honest or not. When I get out of the theatre, you'll have had time to check me out."

Unfortunately, halfway through the movie I had to step out to the men's room. I no sooner got in the men's room than there was that same usher standing right by me. "Okay," he said, "you are either the greatest counterfeit or the greatest con man I've ever met." "Did you check the hotel?" I questioned. "No," he said sternly, "I don't have to. I can spot a con man a mile off." "Look," I said, "here is the $50 bill. You take it, check it out, and when I leave the theatre, give me $45 back please. I want to go in and watch the movie." And I left him with the $50 bill.

When the movie was over, my wife and I walked out and I couldn't find the usher, but I saw a man in a black coat who looked like he was an official. I said to him, "I'm looking for the head usher. He's got my $50 bill." He looked at me and said, "Oh, you're the guy with the $50 bill! We don't take $50 bills here." "Well, I want my change, $45, or I want the $50 bill back," I persisted. Then he reached into his pocket, and with a terrible look on his face he said, "Here is your blankety-blank $50 bill," and he threw it on the floor. So I reached down and picked it up and put it in my pocket. And do you know what? I was mad! Which is not a Christian emotion! Well, I prayed about it, but I was kind of offended.

We walked out of the theatre, and it was raining. We had to walk three blocks to the hotel. My wife said to me, "Bob, this is a great opportunity to practice what you preach. This is loaded with possibilities." "It is?" I said. "Like what?" "Well, let's go back to the hotel, we'll break the bill at the hotel, come back here, pay them the $5, and the usher will listen as we leave a witness for Jesus Christ." We got to the hotel, got change for the $50 bill and walked back to the theatre through the rain. We knocked persistently at the closed door and just kept knocking until the girl who ran the peanut stand opened the door. "Not you again," she said. "Please, can I see the head usher?" I asked.

I went in just in time to see the usher coming down the steps carrying his tuxedo. He was wearing his street clothes. "Oh my God, not you again," he protested. I said, "Yes, it is I again. I have come to pay you the $5 I owe you." "Oh, you didn't have to do that," he said. "I did have to do it," I answered. "I owe it to you. But now you owe me something. I want you to know that I am doing this for one reason: I claim to be a Christian, and it's very exciting trying to follow Christ in daily life. I want you, for the rest of your life, to never forget that if you ever hear people say that Christians are all a bunch of hypocrites, that there's nothing to this Jesus Christ and there's nothing to this God business, I want you never to forget that once there was a man whom you didn't know who came in dripping wet out of the rain to pay his $5 because he said he was a Christian, and that makes a difference." His eyes were moist. He took the $5 and said, "Yes, sir. Thank you, sir. Good night, sir. I'm very sorry." And we smiled and shook hands.

Do you know what it means to forgive? To forgive doesn't just mean that you erase the slate. Forgiveness means you cut the road open and you move back and forth and you help each other. You don't just acquit the person. You see their possibilities and you make them into something beautiful. That can happen to you. But it can only happen when Jesus Christ comes into your life.

I don't think anybody can live in today's world and go through a day, to say nothing of a week or a month, without having the love of Christ in his heart to give the kind of forgiving power we must have today and tomorrow.

CHAPTER SEVEN

Keep
on
Possibilitizing!

"Love endures all things."
(I Cor. 13:7)

7

How You Can Have the Power to Cope

"Love endures all things."

It's a fascinating thing to study human beings!
As a minister - counselor - author I have specialized
in this for nearly a quarter of a century. I can report
to you that, under stress, human beings will usually
react in one of four ways:

(1) Some people will *mope* their way through their troubles. They quickly surrender to self-pity which gives rise to bitterness.

(2) Other people *dope·* their way through; they use narcotics from a bottle, a box, or a bag.

(3) Lots of people just *grope* their way. They get so confused they don't know where they're going. They lose sight of God's plan for their life. So they take their eye off their goal when they start groping.

(4) And some people *hope*. In that hope they find *power to cope*. So they make it!

Now, how do you build your hope so that you can cope? I want to answer that in three words.

I was riding down the freeway the other day and I saw a sign on the back of a vehicle: a sign I have seen on the back of cars, and sweaters of kids in high school. It said, "Keep on Trucking." I really don't know what it means, but I'm going to give you three words that I'd like to make into a bumper sticker! My hope-building three words are: *"Keep on possibilitizing."* Do you know what that means? I don't know what *trucking* means, but I'll tell you what *possibilitizing* means! It is *imagining*, it is *visualizing*, it is *praying*, it is *multiplying* mentally, it is *overcoming*, it is *anticipating*, it is *toughening*, it is *maneuvering*, it is *rebounding* and it is *overpowering* the problem! Let's look at some of these points:

1. *Possibilitizing is imagining*. When God's presence comes into your life through Jesus Christ, Love is going to come into you. This love will so overpower

the negative thoughts that you will be able to possibilitize your way out of your situation. Possibilitizing is imagining that things are going to get better;
they're not going to stay the way they are.

While lecturing in New York I placed a telephone
call to a young woman who told me how she had been
transformed through our Hour of Power ministry.
She said, "A year ago I had major surgery, and it
didn't look like I'd live. I asked my doctor, 'Doctor,
do you think I'll ever walk again?' He looked at me
intently and said, 'That's the wrong question.' I
said, 'I don't think so. I think that's the right question. Do you think I'll ever walk again?' And he answered, 'You're wrong and I'm right. The right question is not do *I* think you'll ever walk again, but do
you think you'll ever walk again?' "

Problems really become serious when they get you
to take your eye off your goal. Constantly imagine
that things will get better. They're not going to stay
the way they are. If you imagine they're going to get
better, you will be in a frame of mind to contribute
to their getting better instead of getting worse.

On a sundial in London, England, is this statement:
"It's always morning somewhere in the world."

2. *Possibilitizing* is visualizing victory beyond the
battle of the hour. It's seeing the victory instead of
the battle. It's seeing the ultimate reward instead of
the pain. It's seeing the crown instead of the cross.

Wesley, that great Methodist minister, was once
talking with a farmer friend out in the country. They
saw a cow with her head over a stone wall, looking

out into the distance. Wesley said to the farmer,
"Suddenly I'm perplexed by a question. Why would
that cow be looking over the wall?" And the farmer
answered, "Well, that's simple: she's looking over the
wall because she can't look through it."

Again and again in your life you're going to have
problems, setbacks, rejections, disappointments, dis-
couragements and prayers that seemingly are not
answered. God may not seem to be around. You may
really hit low. You may even think that prayer
doesn't work and God isn't real and Christ isn't real.
You'll run into a stone wall. When you run into a
stone wall and you can't cope, what do you do? *You
look over it when you can't see through it!*

Keep on possibilitizing!

For years Steve Genter, from Lakewood, California, trained for the Munich Olympics. He wanted to
win so badly in the 200-meter freestyle swim. Some
of you know what happened. One week before the
big event his lung collapsed, and they said that would
wipe him out. But that isn't what he thought. He
looked beyond the moment and over the wall! At his
insistence they cut his chest open, repaired the lung
and stitched him back up. When they called the
names for the event in Munich, Germany, they called
out the name of Steve Genter, and he came up, taped
and stitched! One week after they cut his chest open,
he stood there determined to still try. He was in the
100-meter turn of the 200-meter freestyle event, on
a neck to neck race with Mark Spitz, when he hit
a dead wall, ripped his stitches open! It threw his tim-

ing off, but he kept swimming, and he came in seconds behind Mark Spitz! He came home from the Olympics with a gold medal, a silver medal and a bronze medal!

I've studied the human being and I can tell you that when he looks over the wall to the reward, he'll forget about the pain. Remember, Steve Genter could take no drugs and no medication because that's an Olympics law.

3. *Possibilitizing is praying.* If God has control over your life, He will not let you quit, but He'll keep you in a possibilitizing mood which is praying: "Father, your will be done. This, too, will pass; it cannot last."

A listener to Hour of Power sent me this beautiful poem:

"She used to say to me when things went wrong,
'Why make them worse with worry and regret?
Lift up your heart and join the merry throng
And in the rush of hope you will forget.
Nothing is lasting in this changing sphere.
The troubles that now seem more than you can
    bear
Will all have vanished in another year
Like smoke that melts in the morning air.'
And as I look back now across the years,
I know how very truthfully she spoke.
Time soothes our wounds and stays our falling
    tears,
And from our shoulders lifts the galling yoke.
No sorrow is as lasting as it seems.

The dark cloud that now obscures the gracious day
Will soon be severed by the sun's white beams
And in the glow of noon will fade away."

Keep on praying! After Good Friday comes Easter morning!

4. *Possibilitizing is multiplying the results.* Some of you are tempted to quit because you don't see the returns and the results. We've had Sunday School teachers quit because they didn't think they were doing a good job; they couldn't see the results. I know of ministers who have given up the ministry because they thought they were failing. If only they would keep on possibilitizing! I know salesmen who gave up because they thought they were bombing out. What you should do is possibilitize. That means mentally multiply the possible results!

We're getting ready as a church to celebrate our 20th anniversary . . . 1975 will be our 20th anniversary year, and we're planning fabulous things. I can go back and remember when there was a period of two years when it looked like nothing was happening and everything was sinking. Failure was the only thing that would come our way. But we kept visualizing and we kept imagining and we kept praying, and in our minds we kept multiplying what God could do!

I was inspired by the story of George Smith, the Moravian missionary. All his life he wanted to be a missionary to Africa. He finally finished his preparation and travelled to Africa. He was there but a few months when he was expelled. When he was expelled he left behind only one convert, an old woman. He came back home and soon died, still a young man, literally on his knees praying for Africa, for the people he had come to love. Think of it! All of his life he was preparing . . . he went there . . . spent only a few months . . . came home and died a very young man! *But one hundred years later that mission of one old woman had grown into 13,000 happy, black Christians!*

> ANY FOOL CAN COUNT THE SEEDS
> IN AN APPLE, BUT ONLY GOD CAN
> COUNT THE APPLES IN A SEED.

Possibilitizing — multiply what's going to happen!

Now you can cope when you can imagine that something good will ultimately happen. *So keep on possibilitizing!*

5. *Possibilitizing is overcoming* rather than allowing yourself to be overcome.

I talked on the phone recently to Pat Shaughnessy. Pat is one of the ministers who has been inspired by our possibility thinking. Pat was at the PanAm air counter in August when a bomb went off and killed three people. He suddenly found himself without his leg, blasted off near the hip. When I heard he was still in the hospital, I asked him how he was doing. He laughed at the other end of the line and said, "It's fantastic how God doesn't let anything happen to us unless it's great!" He went on, "You know, Bob, losing a leg isn't that bad. I'm sure people who have never had it happen would say it's impossible to live without a leg. But you know, it isn't so bad. I've got my brain. And I've got my mental attitude straightened out. And guess what? In two weeks I'm going back into the pulpit again, after an absence of nearly three months. I don't know if I'll be preaching in my wheelchair or sitting on a stool, but I'm going to be back, and it's going to be the greatest Sunday in the history of our church." I asked him, "What's the key? What's the real reason you can have such a positive attitude?" And he said, "When you've got Jesus Christ in your heart, then everything else is so exciting that all of the problems you have are really unimportant." So . . .

6. *Possibilitizing is anticipating* that good will come out of this.

Like President Ford's wife said when she went through her surgery. "I'm confident and secure and relaxed, because I believe that God will use this to do a lot of good for a lot of people." And there are a lot of women today who will not die of cancer because they had their examination after President Ford's wife had her surgery.

That's what we call anticipating. In the book of Romans, written by Paul, it says, *"We know that in everything God works for good with those who love him, who are called according to his purpose."* (Rom. 8:28)

7. *Possibilitizing is toughening yourself.* It's keeping up the exercise, it's keeping up the preparation, it's keeping up the training, it's keeping up the working, it's keeping up the studying, it's keeping up the road work: Being tough on yourself. That's what

possibilitizing is. We've never said that possibility thinking makes success cheap and easy. I will tell you this, *no success ideas will work if you don't.*

Now, how do you motivate yourself to keep going in the tough times? Well, let me tell you what has helped me.

I am in a running program, and this morning I frankly didn't feel like running. I thought to myself, "I'll skip today. After all, I've got a full day's work. I have to preach a couple of services and I've some things to do this afternoon and a big meeting tonight, so I think I'll just skip the running today because I really don't feel like it." Then this thought struck me: *All you have to do to be a lasting success is to do what you should when you don't feel like it! If you will do what you should do when you don't feel like it, you'll be doing it all the time because you'll surely do it when you feel like it!* So I went out and ran four miles this morning.

Possibilitizing and possibility thinking is toughening yourself.

I almost never buy clothes. My wife selects most of my clothes, because I don't have the time or the inclination to shop and I'm not that interested in clothes. But I needed a new coat, so I stopped in a store that had a men's half-price sale going on. That kind of motivated me. I went into the shop and saw what I thought was a beautiful coat. It was a green and white plaid. It sounds shocking, I know, but I thought it was nice. I picked out a pair of green pants to go with it, but I think I was looking at the half price more than the match. The owner of the shop said to me, "You know, the green pants don't quite do it." Then he made this statement: "And it would be a pity to miss it when you're so close." So he put the green pants away.

I looked through the whole pile of half-price pants, and I found another pair. I said, "This looks pretty good, don't you think?" "No," the owner said, "it really doesn't. I must say, it's a pity to miss it when you're so close." Then he went through the racks of men's pants that weren't on sale! He picked one out, laid it alongside the green coat and said, "You know, it still doesn't quite do it." So he put the pants back. I said, "How about black? Doesn't black go with everything?" "Oh, I wouldn't like black with it," he replied. And the next thing I knew he took that beautiful green and white plaid sport coat and put it back on the rack and said, "Sorry, I won't sell it to you. I don't have the pants to go with it, and I wouldn't sell it to you if it wouldn't be right." I walked out of there, and all I could think of was what he had said, *"It would be a pity to miss it if you come so close."*

Many of you are tempted to quit. Well, don't give up. *Don't quit when you're so close.* Some of you still, for instance, have one step to take before you have success. I'm thinking of some of you spiritually. Wouldn't it be a tragedy to come to the end of your life and have somebody say about you: "It's a pity that he missed it. He came so close! He quit just before he would have made it!"

The real power behind possibilitizing is the power from God Himself that comes into a human life when that life accepts Jesus Christ as its Saviour and Lord. And some of you have not done that. Simply receive Christ into your life by faith. He's alive. He can change you. He lives within me. I have a relationship with Him. I know He has saved me from my sins. I know the worst that could happen is I'd die. But when that happens I will be born again into eternal life, because He's my Saviour. I've come so close and I won't miss it, because He will never let me down. He won't let you down, either.

Do you want to have power to cope? Get Christ's love in your life, because God's love is the love that endures all things.

Saint Paul did it. He received Christ into his life and amazing power came in! "I can do all things through Christ who strengthens me." (*Phil. 4:13*)

Listen: If you never have before — then this moment receive Christ into your life. Feel His love flow in. Feel the Spiritual Power! You'll start moving . . . you'll possibilitize! You'll overcome!

CHAPTER EIGHT

You need me, therefore I love you. This is Christian Love.

"There is no fear in love."
(I John 4:18)

8

Love Conquers Fear

"There is no fear in love."

Wouldn't it be wonderful if something happened deep within your mind to give you such inner confidence, security and calmness that you would never be afraid of anybody or anything ever again? Wouldn't it be fantastic if you had a mental and spiritual experience that would permanently give you an imperishable and invisible shield against anxiety, worry, fear and guilt? The truth is, if you have an experience with Perfect Love, you will conquer fear in your life *forever*."

> "*There is no fear in love, for perfect*
> *love casts out fear.*" (I John 4:18)

What is very important is that we understand that there is such a thing as *imperfect* love and there is such a thing as *perfect* love. All doctrines, all lectures, all sermons, all messages, all books, all songs that talk about love are imperfect. And that's part of our problem in the world today. Much of what we think of as love is imperfect love. Consider this: There are three levels of love:

No. 1: "*I love you because I need you.*" This is imperfect love. It is basically selfish.

No. 2: "*I love you because I want you.*" This may be nothing more than lust.

No. 3: "*I love you because you need me.*" *I need to give myself away to people who need help. You need me, therefore I love you.*" This is Christian love.

Look at these three statements and you will see the difference between counterfeit and authentic love; between imperfect and perfect love.

"*I need to give myself away to people who need help. You need me, therefore I love you.*" This is the essence of perfect love. Where do you find it?

Recently I passed through one of our great mid-America airports. I had just delivered a lecture at a college where they required all the students on the campus to read my book entitled, "Self-Love, the Dynamic Force of Success." I was asked to deliver a lecture on the subject, and answer questions from the student body. It was one of those quick 24-hour, out-of-town trips. As I was returning through this airport I stopped, as I often do, at a candy store. It was the Fannie Mae Candy Store.

I must hasten to say that I don't like candy. I used to like it, but I have psyched myself out because I've decided that the only way to lose weight is not to diet. Do you know what a diet is? A diet is when you deprive yourself of something you want to reach an objective, at which point you reward yourself by giving yourself what you've denied yourself all the time. So I decided the only way to lose weight, and keep it off, was to lose my appetite for foods that would make me fat. So I programmed myself (I think) not to like candy. I tell myself that the chocolate is either too bitter or it's too ghastly sweet. And if that doesn't work I imagine that their creamy contents were probably put together under unsanitary conditions.

At any rate, I go through this whole mental rigmarole to convince myself that I can't stand candy. But I stopped in to buy chocolates for my wife; she loves chocolates. She happens to particularly love chocolate-covered nuts. So I walked into this Fannie Mae Store where a clerk in a white dress greeted me from behind the counter. There was another customer at the counter, an older woman, in a red dress with a flight bag and a little suitcase. She seemed to be indecisively window shopping. The woman in

white wasn't doing anything to help her, so I said,
"Do you have one-pound boxes of chocolate-covered
nuts?" And at that point the customer said, "Oh, sure
they've got one-pound boxes of all kinds of chocolate-
covered nuts." I looked back at the clerk who was after
all the real authority. She could see that I was waiting
for her to answer. "Yes, we can make up a one-pound
box of all kinds of chocolate-covered nuts." "Maybe
you have a one-pound box of turtles, chocolate-
covered nuts with caramel?" I asked. The customer
interrupted again, "Yes, they have those in one-pound
boxes. They also have those in three-pound boxes!"
I looked at the clerk, waiting for the reply from the
real authority (not content with the doubtful opin-
ion of just another plain customer!) The clerk looked
nervously at the customer who kept interrupting and
finally said, "Yes, we do have them in one-pound
boxes. We also have them in three-pound boxes."
Again she looked nervously at the customer. And
again this customer intruded with the unsolicited
advice: "But I recommend you take the one-pound
box of the Colonial. It's got creams in it, too!"

The clerk on the other side of the counter said,
"Yes, why don't you try the one with the creams?
The Colonial is really a very good box!" I thought to
myself, "Who is working for whom around here?"
It really became quite exasperating. "How much is
the Colonial box?" I asked. The clerk told me how
much it was, and then the customer came back and
said, "Really, their Colonial box has got everything.
It's got chocolate turtles, chocolate-covered nuts,

cashews, walnuts and peanuts," adding enthusiastical-
ly, "they're beautifully packaged, too!" Just then she
said, "Oh, I've got to go or I'll miss my plane," and
she picked up her bag and left. Both the clerk and I
breathed sighs of relief to see her leave.

Immediately the clerk in the white dress turned
around and called, "Okay, girls, you can come out
now. Fannie Mae is gone!" "You're kidding!" I gasped.
"Oh, no," she said. "That's Fannie Mae. Well, that's
not her real name, but when she married her husband
and he died and left her the candy store, she decided
she was going to make something of her life. She put
together some new recipes and packaged some new
candies and now has 117 stores all up and down the
United States! She calls them her 117 children, and
all she does is fly around to visit the stores."

She was the authority, and I wasn't even listening
to her! She knew the recipes, she put the whole thing
together, and I was foolishly looking to some clerk
as the authority — a clerk who probably never made
a chocolate in her life!

If you want to know about love, then listen to the
real authority, Jesus Christ! Ministers, priests and
psychologists at best are clerks. We can only take the
concept and give it to you. But we don't manufac-
ture it! We don't create it. All the while, maybe
through sermons, songs or people who write litera-
ture, Jesus Christ is coming to you, and you consider
Him an intruder and are vastly relieved when He gets
out and leaves you alone. Go to the authority! The
real authority is Jesus Christ. He is perfect love!

"Perfect love casts out fear." Christ is perfect love. In other words, when Jesus Christ comes into your life, I won't have to tell you what love is. You will know from personal experience! And that's the only way to know. There is a hymn that closes with the lines, "The love of Jesus, what it is, none but His loved ones know." It's not something you can be *taught,* it has to be *caught.*

I like the lesson I learned from Frank Laubach: "None of us loves perfectly, but Christ loves perfectly. No human being is totally perfect in love, but Christ is. Now, let's suppose you run into somebody you can't love. What do you do? Do you let yourself hate them? No. Do you tell yourself, 'I'm a Christian, therefore I'm going to love them.' Yes. Tell yourself that, *but it might not work.* Be realistic. What do you do? Surrender to your negative thoughts about the person? Of course not. You call in the expert, the authority, Jesus Christ."

Here's how Laubach taught us how to handle the situation: "Put one hand up in the air, open your palm and stretch the other hand out with a pointed finger aimed at your adversary. Now pray: 'Jesus Christ, you are perfect love. I am imperfect love. Because I'm imperfect I can't love that guy.' (Keep your finger pointed right at him! Aim at his heart. Aim at his head.) Pray: 'Jesus Christ, will you please fall into the palm of my hand, flow down through my arm, through my elbow, through my shoulder, my chest, my heart, down my other arm, out of the end of my finger, and hit him, please? Hit him hard!

Hit him gently! Hit him beautifully! You love him,
Jesus! You can do it! I can't do it! But *you* can!' "

I gave that lesson some years ago in this church.
One man who heard me thought to himself: "Boy,
Schuller's getting carried away again." He said to me
a week later, "Dr. Schuller, guess what happened?
Monday morning I went to work remembering your
sermon of the day before. The first person I saw coming into my store was the one salesman I could not
stand! I saw him drive up to the curb; I knew his
car. I saw him get out of that car. And I was already
in a bad mood! My secretary, who also goes to this
church and heard the same sermon I heard, said to
me, 'Maybe you'd better try what Dr. Schuller talked
about yesterday. Shoot him with prayers.' So before
he got in I reached one hand in the air and with the
other hand I pointed at him through the window. He
was gawking at me as if I was nuts.

"Later on he told me he thought I was going to
change a light bulb. But I said, 'Jesus, I can't love that
guy. I can't stomach him, to say nothing of loving
him. But *you* can. Flow into my hand, through my
arm, through my heart, and *you* love him, Jesus.'
And the most amazing thing happened. I couldn't
believe it. When the man came up to me and said,
'Good morning. How are you today?' — and I've
never heard him say it that way before — I looked at
his face and saw that it had a countenance about it
that I never saw before. His eyes, that always looked
so nasty, now looked so sweet. It worked! *I ended up
loving this guy!*"

"Perfect love casts out fear." It casts out all kinds of negative forces. Perfect love is Christ flowing through you. Christ is perfect love. So the secret, of course, is to have a personal relationship with Christ. And this is possible!

Why does it cast out fear? For one simple reason: Selfish love always produces fear. If I love you because I need you, or I love you because I want you, I'm going to be afraid that I might not get you, and then I'll have lost something that I wanted to gain. But if you love because you want to give something to somebody, you'll never become fearful or worried or tense. For *a giving love can never lose: If they take what you offer, you'll succeed! . . . and if they don't take it, you've still got it! Either way, you can't lose!* So there will be no subliminal anxieties or fears of being rejected or hurt.

Selfish love is the kind of love that builds walls more than it builds bridges.

It reminds me of what Robert Frost once said, "Before you build walls, make sure you know what you're walling out and what you're walling in."

About a month ago I was in St. Louis, Missouri, where I was to give a lecture. It was four o'clock in the afternoon, and I was to give my lecture in the main hall that night. So I unpacked my suitcase and pulled on the grey suit that I was going to wear for my lecture, just to make sure it was in good shape. Then I made this discovery: I hadn't worn the suit for four months and in the meantime I had lost 36 pounds. So the trousers were way too big for me.

Unfortunately, they were trousers that didn't have loops for a belt.

Now you talk about being nervous! To be a lecturer on a platform in a pair of pants that are a 42 when you wear a 38! — I had a problem! I knew I either had to get a very hefty safety pin or I needed some emergency tailoring done in a hurry. I called the desk in the hotel. They told me no tailor could do it in such a short time. But they said, "You can always go to Mr. Harris. Maybe he could do it." So I went down to Harris the Tailor in the mall in downtown St. Louis, three blocks away. There I met one of the most marvelous of men, Mr. Harris, a seasoned gentleman, who really knew his business. "Sir, can you take my trousers in about four inches?" I asked. "Well, that'll take about two hours," he answered. I looked him right in the eye and said, "Sir, aren't you Mr. Harris?" "Yes," he said, and I continued. "Well, I was told you're the best tailor in town." "Well, ah, . . . " he hesitated. I went on, "I happen to know a tailor in Los Angeles who could do it in twenty minutes. And I'm sure you're better than he is." He just stared at me. And I stared at him, because I needed the job done. He finally said, "Okay, go to that little room there and throw me your trousers."

I walked into the room, carrying a book I had just bought, when Mr. Haris asked, "What's the name of that book you've got?" "Loneliness, the Fear of Love," I told him. "Well, you're going to get awful lonely in there waiting for these pants to get done," he said. "Oh, I don't think I'll get lonely," I replied. "I never get lonely, because I've got a friend who is with me." Seventeen minutes later my trousers were back with the best job of tailoring I've ever seen!

"Are you a minister or something?" Mr. Harris asked. "You look a little familiar." "Yes, sir, I am," I told him. "What kind of religion do you have? What is your faith?" he asked. "I'm glad you asked that, Mr. Harris," I said. "What does my faith mean to me? Well, it's not a *religion*. By that I mean simply a course like psychology, sociology, anthropology, biology or chemistry. It's not a religion — like some spiritual kind of philosophy. And it's not a set of *restrictions*. 'Don't do this, don't do that.' And it's not a list of *resolutions*. 'I'm going to do this, I'm going to do that.' And it's not a *ritual*. 'Now we pray, now we bow our heads, now we give the offering. Now we read the Bible.' No, my faith is a *relationship*. I have a friend, and He's Jesus Christ! I have received Him into my life, and I feel that within myself there is a Love that never leaves me. That's a love that conquers my fear. I'm not afraid to die tonight, because I know that I won't go to hell, I'll go to heaven. I have a Saviour. So the ultimate fear is flushed out! Because He died on a cross for me and He has scars to prove it!"

I invite you now to receive Jesus Christ into your life by faith. Then a Love will come into your life that will give you amazing peace of mind! And when that happens you've really found the answer to a love that drives out loneliness forever.

Love — or loneliness — you decide!

Choose love — by choosing to receive Jesus Christ into your life . . . *NOW!*